H. T. Banks

The Visitors' Centennial Guide to the Capitol

Gives a Brief History of the Capitol, Together with a Specific Description...

H. T. Banks

The Visitors' Centennial Guide to the Capitol
Gives a Brief History of the Capitol, Together with a Specific Description...

ISBN/EAN: 9783337161132

Printed in Europe, USA, Canada, Australia, Japan

Cover: Foto ©ninafisch / pixelio.de

More available books at **www.hansebooks.com**

The Visitors' Centennial Guide

TO THE

CAPITOL.

—— ··❖·· ——

GIVES A BRIEF HISTORY OF THE CAPITOL, TO-
GETHER WITH A SPECIFIC DESCRIPTION OF
ALL ITS PARTS, A LIST OF SENATORS,
REPRESENTATIVES, AND DELE-
GATES, AND DIRECTIONS
TO THE PRINCIPAL BUILDINGS IN THE CITY.

——— ◆ ———

PRICE FIFTEEN CENTS.

◆

Entered according to Act of Congress by H. T. BANKS, in the year 1876,
in the Office of the Librarian of Congress at Washington.

——— ◆ ———

WASHINGTON, D. C.:
R. BERESFORD, PRINTER, 523 SEVENTH ST., N. W.
1876.

THE CAPITOL.

THE CAPITOL

of the United States, the most beautiful, magnificent and superb structure of the kind ever erected by human hands, rears its lofty pinnacle far above the surrounding steeples and spires of Washington City; and, situated upon a high and elevated site, ninety feet above the bosom of the Potomac, majestically stands the peer in architectural design of beauty, stability and advantage of natural scenery.

In the year 1790 President Washington advised the removal of the Capital from Philadelphia to the place it now occupies on the east bank of the Potomac, and in September, 1793, he, with his own hands, laid the foundation stone of the main or original building. The British in 1814 destroyed each wing, and in 1818 the rebuilding commenced, which was finished during the summer of 1827, though the present cast iron dome was not completed until 1865, a small, temporary wooden structure occupying its place until that time.

The present north and south wings were begun July 4, 1851, and completed in 1867.

The centre building is constructed of sandstone; the wings and connections of white marble.

The building, measuring north and south, is 751 feet; the greatest depth east and west, 324 feet, and the height, from the level of the grounds to the top of the dome, is 396 feet.

It was intended that the city should be built on the plateau east of the Capitol, conseqently the architect fronted the building in that direction; but real estate owners, demanding such exhorbitant prices for their property, caused the city to be located on the lower and cheaper land west and northwest.

On the grounds directly in front of the main building is Greenough's grand collossal statue of Washington, the entire cost of which was $44,000.

As we pass up the steps leading to the

EASTERN PORTICO,

which is 160 feet in length, we are attracted by the group of statues crowning the abutments on either side, the one on the left representing the Discovery of America. This group is by Persico, and cost $24,000 and five years' labor.

The one on the right represents Civilization, or

the first settlement in the New World. This is by Greenough, and cost $24,000 and the labor of twelve years.

Upon the portico, in niches on each side of the main door, are the statues of Peace and War. Smiling Peace offers the olive branch to savage War on the opposite side.

At the east door leading into the Rotunda we find the renowned

ROGERS' BRONZE DOOR,

the handsomest in the world. It was modeled by Randolph Rogers, in Rome, 1858, and cast in bronze by F. V. Miller, in Munich, 1860. It weighs 20,000 pounds and was purchased for $28,000. It consists of two leaves, upon the panels of which are represented leading events in the life of Columbus, which, beginning with the lower panel on the right leaf, are as follows:

1. Columbus before the Court of Salamanca explaining his plans and theory.

2. Departure of Columbus from Palos to visit the Spanish Court.

3. Columbus presenting his plans to Ferdinand and Isabella.

4. Columbus leaving Palos on his first voyage in seek of the New World.

5. Encounter with the natives.

6. Welcome of Columbus at Barcelona.

7. Columbus in chains.

8. Death óf Columbus at Valladolid, May 20, 1506.

On the transom of the door is represented Columbus landing on the Island of San Salvador. On the casing over this is a head of Columbus, and at the top and bottom on each side is a statuette, those on the right representing Asia and Europe, and on the left Africa and America.

The small niches in the frame on either side of the panels contain statuettes of the friends and associates of Columbus, as follows: Alexander VI, Pedro Gonzales de Mendoza, King Ferdinand, Queen Isabella, King Charles VIII, Beatriz de Bobadilla, King John II, King Henry VII, Juan Perez de Marchena, Martin Alonzo Pinzon, Hernando Cortez, Bartholomew Columbus, Alonzo de Ojeda, Vasco Nuñez de Balboa, Amerigo Vespucci, Francisco Pazarro.

After passing through the Bronze Door we enter

THE ROTUNDA,

which is the center of the building, and roofed by the largest dome in the New World. The diameter at the base is 96 feet, and the distance from the floor to the fresco overhead is 180 feet. Commencing at the right, as we enter through the Bronze Door and proceeding around the circle, we find a series of historical paintings, by the most eminent artists of the profession.

1. *The Landing of Columbus*, October 12, 1492; by Vanderlyn. An appropriation of $10,000 was made for this painting in 1842.

2. *Embarkation of the Pilgrims* from Holland, July 22, 1620; by Weir. Purchased in 1836 at a cost of $10,000.

3. *Resignation of General Washington* at Annapolis, December 23, 1783; by Trumbull, 1817. Cost $8,000

4. *Surrender of Lord Cornwallis* to General Lincoln, Yorktown, October 19, 1781; by Trumbull. Cost $8,000.

5. *Surrender of Burgoyne* to General Gates, Saratoga, October 17, 1777; by Trumbull. Cost $8,0 0.

6. *Declaration of Independence*, Philadelphia, July 4, 1776; by Trumbull. Cost $8,000.

7. *Baptism of Pocahontas* at Jamestown, Va., 1613; by Chapman. Cost $10,000.

8. *Discovery of the Mississippi River* by De Soto, May, 1541. This painting was ordered from Powell in 1850 at a cost of $12,000.

We have now examined these magnificent types of the art, eight in all, that so becomingly adorn the panels in the Rotunda set apart for their exhibition ; and on the wall over the first one on the right and left of the east and west doors are busts, underneath of which we at once recognize the names most prominent in the participations of government, recorded in the early history of our New World—*Cabot*, *Columbus*, *Raleigh* and *La Salle*.

Then over each door or entrance we find, in *basso relievo*, caricatures, representing, first over the east door, *The Landing of the Pilgrims* in 1620; by Cauciei.

Over the north door, *Penn's Treaty with the Indians* under the elm, 1621; by Gevelot.

West door, *Pocahontas Saving the Life of John Smith*, 1606; by Capellano.

South door, *Daniel Boone in Conflict with the Indians*, 1773; by Cauciei.

The cost of these four pieces of sculpture was $14,000.

Passing through the north entrance to the Rotunda, to the first door on the left, we come to stairway leading to

THE DOME, BATTERY AND ELECTRICIAN'S ROOM.

The last two we find at the head of the first steps to the right, and proceeding through the door on the left, we, after some exertion, and resting on the different landings, at last reach the platform or "whispering gallery," immediately beneath the wonderful and magnificent fresco by Brumidi. The center and crowning figure of this painting is a deification of *"Pater Patriœ,"* WASHINGTON, while on his right we recognize FREEDOM, and on his left VICTORY. Around the group, in semi circle form, are thirteen virgins, one for each State represented in the Continental Congress, and woven in their hair are leaves, emblematic and characteristic of the State they represent. Stamped upon the banner they wave is the motto of the Union— "E Pluribus Unum." There are also represented upon the canopy, beginning at the west :

1. *The Fall of Tyranny.*
2. *Agriculture.*
3. *Mechanics.*
4. *Commerce.*
5. *Marine.*
6. *Arts and Sciences.*

Brumidi accomplished this grand and unsurpassed piece of work in 1864, for which he received the compensation of $40,000. After viewing this painting we pass up another flight of steps, which lands us on the top of the Dome, where we are more than paid for the labor and exertion of ascending by the excellent bird's eye view of the city we have before us.

The entire dome is of cast iron, and weighs 8,909,200 pounds. Upon the apex stands a bronze statue of FREEDOM, which is nineteen feet high, and weighs nearly 15,000 pounds.

Through the western entrance to the Rotunda (opposite the Bronze Door) we pass to the

CONGRESSIONAL LIBRARY,

which contains about 300,000 volumes. Two copies of every book published in the United States are required to be deposited in this Library. This is a place which every visitor to the Capitol should see. Any person with an order from either a Senator, Congressman, judge of the Supreme Court or head of a Department is entitled to obtain and read any work which may be in the Library.

Proceeding through the north door of the Rotunda, we reach, on the right, a flight of steps —opposite those leading to the Dome—connecting the first and second stories of the building; and then on a little further we arrive at the

UNITED STATES SUPREME COURT ROOM,

which was used as the Senate Chamber until

1859, and during which time the Supreme Court occupied the room beneath, now used as the

LAW LIBRARY,

the entrance to which is found at the foot of the stairway just mentioned above; and at the head of this stairway we find an entrance to the

MARSHAL'S OFFICE OF THE SUPREME COURT.

Immediately across the corridor from the court room is the

OFFICE OF THE CLERK OF THE SUPREME COURT.

After leaving the Supreme Court room and proceeding north through the corridor we are led to the main entrance to the floor of the

SENATE CHAMBER,

when continuing to the left through the corridor we reach the eastern

STAIRWAY LEADING TO THE GALLERY OF THE SENATE.

Before making the ascent the visitor will be attracted by a large marble statue of Franklin, the work of Powers, which occupies a niche just at the foot of the steps. Cost, $10,000. Opposite this statue, over the first landing of the staircase, is Powell's grand painting of

PERRY'S VICTORY ON LAKE ERIE,

which cost $25,000.

Continuing up the staircase and turning to the right we reach the

LADIES' GALLERY,

and in the vestibule leading to which are two magnificent paintings by Thomas Moran, representing

THE CAÑON OF THE YELLOWSTONE
and
THE CAÑON OF THE COLORADO.

The Senate Chamber is 113 feet long, 80 feet wide and 36 feet high. On the east, south and west are cloak rooms for the use of the Senators, connected with the floor of the Chamber, and on the north is the lobby. Directly over these are the galleries, arranged as follows: Over the President's chair is set apart for newspaper reporters, on the east for ladies, west for gentlemen, and opposite the President's chair is the

DIPLOMATIC GALLERY.

The western staircase to the Senate gallery is of white marble. Just above the first landing is a very handsome painting by Walker, representing the

STORMING OF CHAPULTEPEC

in 1847 by the American army under General
Scott; cost, $6,000. And at the foot of the
steps, in a niche, similar to the one at the eastern stairway, is a statue in marble of *John Hancock*, President of the Continental Congress, 1776.

The visitor, after passing the eastern staircase
and the statue of Franklin, will enter the corridor leading to the famous

CRAWFORD BRONZE DOOR,

which is divided into two leaves, just as the
Rodgers Door, at the east entrance to the Rotunda, and contains six panels, on which are
scenes representing events during the Revolutionary War. Beginning at the top panel on
the left and continuing in succession we find:

1. *Battle of Bunker Hill and Death of Warren*, June 17, 1775.

2. *Battle of Monmouth*, June, 1778.

3. *Battle of Yorktown*, October 19, 1781.

4. *Washington at Trenton*, April, 1789, on his way to assume the office of President of the United States.

5. *Inauguration of Washington*, April 30, 1789.

6. *Washington Laying the Corner-stone of the Capitol at Washington*, September 18, 1793.

As we enter this door immediately to the right
is found the

SENATE POST OFFICE,

which is elegantly frescoed and becomingly decorated. Passing through the north door of the
Post Office we enter the

SERGEANT-AT-ARMS' OFFICE,

also handsomely frescoed, as is the

SENATE RECEPTION ROOM,

which we find adjoining the Post Office on the
west. On the south wall of the room is an oil
painting of Washington, Jefferson and Hamilton.

Leaving this room through the west door, we
pass the magnificent

BRONZE STAIRCASE,

leading to the floor below, and then enter the

SENATE LOBBY,

from which we find an entrance to the

VICE PRESIDENT'S ROOM,

(which is through the first door on the right as
we enter the lobby,)

MARBLE ROOM

and

PRESIDENT'S ROOM,

which, however, is seldom used by the President
himself, and through the kindness of the Sergeant-

at-Arms or one of his assistants visitors can be admitted any day except Sunday. The walls, ceiling and floor of this room are all handsomely and elegantly decorated. On the ceiling in fresco we find likenesses of Columbus, William Brewster, Americus Vespucius and Benjamin Franklin. On the walls are portraits of Washington, Thomas Jefferson, Henry Knox, Alexander Hamilton, Edmund Randolph and S. Osgood, and the floor is carpeted with a rich carmine velvet carpet, in one piece, and made expressly in Scotland for this room. The fresco work on the walls and ceiling, as well as that in the entire Senate wing, is by Brumidi.

Leaving the Senate Chamber and passing south through the Rotunda we find the

STATUARY HALL,

which was used as the Hall of Representatives until 1860, and in 1864 was set apart for a National Statuary Hall, where each State is requested to deposit statues of two of its most distinguished and lamented citizens. The following States have to this time contributed :

VERMONT—*Ethan Allen.*
MASSACHUSETTS—*John Winthrop and Samuel Adams.*
CONNECTICUT—*Jonathan Trumbull and Roger Sherman.*

RHODE ISLAND—*Nathaniel Greene and Roger Williams.*
NEW YORK—*George Clinton and R. R. Livingston.*
OREGON—*E. D. Baker.*

Besides these the Hall contains a plaster cast
of the statue of *Washington,* by Houdon, 1788;
a bust of *Lincoln,* by Mrs. Ames, and a statue of
the same by Miss Vinnie Ream; a bust of *Kos-
ciusko,* by Saunders; a statue of *Alexander Hamilton,* by Stone, and a bust of *Thomas Crawford,*
sculptor. Over the north door is noticeable a
very elegant clock encased in white marble,
which has timed the remarks of Webster, Clay,
Calhoun, Cass, Corwine and hundreds of others,
and also counted the seconds as Prentiss spoke
the eloquent and undying words of his renowned
Mississippi contested election speech.

Passing through the south door of the Statuary
Hall we enter the connection which joins the House
of Representatives, or the south wing to the main
building, and which leads us to the principle entrance to the Hall of Representatives. Reaching
the main door of the Hall and turning to the
right we come to the western staircase leading to
the

LADIES' AND MEMBERS' GALLERY.

At the base of the steps we find a bust, in
bronze, of the Indian chief, *Bee-she-kee,* the Buf-

falo; and opposite on the wall is Leutz's cele-
brated chromo-silica,

WESTWARD HO!

and immediately below, encased in the same bor-
der, is Bierstadt's *"Golden Gate,"* or entrance to
San Francisco harbor. On the north side of the
painting is a portrait of *Daniel Boone,* while
opposite is one of *Captain Clark.*

Upon reaching the gallery floor we find first,
the *Members',* the *Diplomatic,* then the *Ladies'*
gallery, these being on the west side of the Hall,
and from which we have a good view of the

HALL OF REPRESENTATIVES,

which is 139 feet long by 93 feet wide; the floor
is 113 feet long by 67 feet wide. The Speaker's,
Clerks' and Official Reporters' desks are of white
marble. On the right of the Speaker is a very
fine portrait of Washington, and a painting by
Bierstadt, representing the "King's River Cañon;"
while on the west, or left of the Speaker, is the
portrait of LaFayette, presented by himself to
Congress while on his last visit to this country;
and adjoining this is the "Discovery of the Hud-
son," and still further on is a fresco by Brumidi,
representing Washington at Yorktown.

The Hall is lighted, heated and ventilated by the same means as the Senate, though on a larger scale. At the foot of the eastern staircase leading to the gallery we find a marble statue of Jefferson, by Powers; cost, $10,000. And over the first landing is a very fine equestrian portrait of Winfield Scott, by Troga.

THE HEATING AND VENTILATING APPARATUS
of the House is in the basement, and is reached by a staircase leading from the corridor on the left of the foot of the western stairway of the House wing.

THE CRYPT
is under the Rotunda, and is reached by stairways leading from the corridors just after passing through the north and south doors of the Rotunda, and also by a passage-way at the foot of the main, or western, staircase, which leads to the Rotunda, and is connected with the north and south wings by means of corridors. In the Crypt are 40 columns which support the floor of the Rotunda.

THE UNDERCRAFT
is beneath the Crypt, and was intended as the tomb of Washington. Here can be found the bier which held the remains of Lincoln, Chase

and Thaddeus Stevens. On a trip to this place the visitor should be accompanied by an officer of the building.

THE COURT OF CLAIMS

occupies the rooms at the foot and on the right of the western staircase leading from the Rotunda; and opposite, on the left, is found the Committee Rooms of the House, on Mines and Mining, Territorial Delegates, Education and Labor, and Revision of the Laws.

The House Committee on Banking and Currency occupy the room adjoining the Stationery Room of the House, the entrance to which is from the Statuary Hall, opposite the House Document Room.

Rooms located on first floor, or basement of Senate Wing.

Senate Committee on Patents.
Senate Committee on Post Offices and Post Roads.
Senate Committee on Foreign Relations.
Superintendent of the Senate Folding-Room.
Senate Committee on Contingent Expenses.
Senate Committee on Agriculture.
Senate Stationery Room.
Senate Committee on Territories.
Senate Committee on the Judiciary.
Senate Committee on Naval Affairs.
Senate Committee on Military Affairs.
Senate Committee on the Library.
Senate Committee on the District of Columbia.
Senate Committee on Revision of the Laws.
Senate Committee on Indian Affairs.
Senate Committee on Rules.
Senate Committee on Enrolled Bills.
Senate Restaurant.
Senate Committee on Public Lands.
Senate Committee on Education and Labor.
Senate Committee on Pensions.

Rooms on second or main floor of Senate Wing.

Senate Post Office.
Office of the Sergeant-at-Arms of the Senate.

Senate Reception Room.
Vice-President's Room.
Marble Room.
President's Room.
Senate Committee on Manufacturers.
Senate Committee on Appropriations.
Executive, Financial and Chief Clerk's Rooms.
Office of the Secretary of the Senate.
Senate Committee on Finance.
Senate Official Reporters.

Rooms on third or gallery floor of Senate Wing.

Joint Committees on Public Printing.
Senate Committee on Revolutionary Claims.
Senate Committee on Claims.
Senate Committee on Private Land Claims.
Ladies' Retiring Room.
Senate Committee on Mines and Mining.
Senate Committee on Commerce.
Senate Committee on Privileges and Elections.
Senate Committee on Railroads and Transportation.
Senate Committee on Public Buildings and Grounds.
Senate Document Room.

Rooms located on first or basement floor of the House of Representatives, or South Wing.

House Post Office.
House Committee on Public Buildings and Grounds.

House Committee on Territories.

House Official Reporters.

House Committee on Expenditures in the War Department.

House Committee on Public Expenditures and Private Land Claims.

Doorkeeper's Room.

House Index Room.

House Committee on Invalid Pensions.

House Committee on Claims.

House Committee on Agriculture and Manufactures.

House Committee on War Claims.

House Committee on Accounts.

House Committee on Indian Affairs.

House Committee on Printing.

House Committee on Post Offices and Post Roads.

House Restaurant.

Rooms on second or main floor of House Wing.

House Committee on Naval Affairs.

House File Clerk's Room.

Office Clerk of the House.

Speaker's Room.

House Reception Room.

Office Sergeant-at-Arms of the House.

House Official Reporter's Room.

House Committee on Appropriations.

House Committee on Ways and Means.

House Committee on Military Affairs.

Rooms on third or attic floor of House Wing.

House Committee on District of Columbia.
House Committee on Roads and Canals, and Patents.
House Committee on Elections.
House Committee on Pensions and Pacific Railroad.
Ladies' Retiring Room.
House Committee on Public Lands.
House Committee on Commerce.
House Committee on the Judiciary.
House Committee on Foreign Relations.
House Library.
House Committee on Mileage and Militia.

ALPHABETICAL LIST OF SENATORS, WITH THEIR RESIDENCES IN WASHINGTON.

T. W. FERRY, President...............National Hotel.
Alcorn, James L., Mississippi.........1212 G street, N. W.
Allison, William B., Iowa ....Wormley's, 15th and H sts.
Anthony, Henry B., Rhode Island...1402 H street, N. W.
Barnum, William H., Connecticut...Arlington Hotel.
Bayard, Thomas F., Delaware..........1413 Massachusetts avenue.
Blaine, James G., Maine................821 15th street, N. W.
Bogy, Lewis V., Missouri...............406 6th street, N. W.
Booth, Newton, California..............601 13th street, N. W.
Boutwell, George S., Massachusetts..1100 Vermont avenue, N. W.
Bruce, Blanche K., Mississippi.......316 A street, N. E.
Burnside, Ambrose E., Rhode Isl'd..1823 H street, N. W.
Cameron, Angus, Wisconsin...... 810 12th street, N. W.
Cameron, Simon, Pennsylvania ......Congressional Hotel.
Caperton, Allen T., West Virginia...1412 I street, N. W.
Christiancy, Isaac P., Michigan ......310 Indiana avenue, N. W.
Clayton, Powell, Arkansas............512 13th street, N. W.
Cockrell, Francis M., Missouri........320 8th street, N. W.
Conkling, Roscoe, New York..........Wormley's, 15th and H sts.
Conover, Simon B., Florida............722 21st street, N. W.
Cooper, Henry, Tennessee ....1412 I street, N. W.
Cragin, Aaron H., New Hampshire..325 East Capitol street.
Davis, Henry G., West Virginia......Riggs House.
Dawes, Henry L., Massachusetts.....1213 K street, N. W.
Dennis, George R., Maryland...........1303 F street, N. W.
Dorsey, S. W., Arkansas................1312 F street, N. W.
Eaton, William W., Connecticut.....1405 I street, N. W.
Edmunds, George F., Vermont........1411 Massachusetts avenue.
Frelinghuysen, F. T., New Jersey...1731 I street, N. W.
Goldthwaite, George, Alabama.........413 4th street, N. W.
Gordon, John B., Georgia...............Gay and Congress sts., Geo'n.
Hamilton, Morgan C., Texas............227 Delaware avenue.
Hamlin, Hannibal, Maine...............113 Maryland avenue, N. E.
Harvey, James M., Kansas ....607 13th street, N. W.
Hitchcock, Phineas W., Nebraska...610 14th street, N. W.
Howe, Timothy O., Wisconsin.........1708 I street, N. W.
Ingalls, John J., Kansas................1311 H street, N. W.
Johnston, John W., Virginia...........508 12th street, N. W.
Jones, Charles W., Florida ....417 New Jersey ave., S. E.
Jones, John P., Nevada..................N. J. ave., and B st. south.
Kelly, James K., Oregon.................337 C street, N. W.
Kernan, Francis, New York............Arlington Hotel.
Key, David M., Tennessee..............903 E street, N. W.

Logan, John A., Illinois................808 12th street, N. W.
McCreery, Thomas C., Kentucky.....Union Hotel, Georgetown.
McDonald, Joseph E., Indiana........1221 G street, N. W.
McMillan, Samuel J. R., Minnesota-911 New York avenue.
Maxey, Samuel B., Texas................1412 I street, N. W.
Merrimon, A. S., North Carolina.....1321 New York avenue.
Mitchell, John H., Oregon........ -- 1607 I street, N. W.
Morrill, Justin S., Vermont.............Vermont ave. and M street.
Morton, Oliver P., Indiana ....Ebbitt House.
Norwood, Thomas M., Georgia ....2100 H street, N. W.
Oglesby, Richard J., Illinois............1304 F street, N. W.
Paddock, Algernon S., Nebraska.....1712 L street, N. W.
Patterson, John J., South Carolina-1331 11th street, N. W.
Randolph, Theo. F., New Jersey.......Arlington Hotel.
Ransom, Matt. W., North Carolina.508 11th street. N. W.
Robertson, Thos. J., South Carolina-1401 K street. N. W.
Sargent, Aaron A., California............Conn. ave. and DeSales st.
Saulsbury, Eli, Delaware ....510 12th street, N. W.
Sharon, William, Nevada ....Arlington Hotel.
Sherman, John, Ohio....................1323 K street, N. W.
Spencer, George E., Alabama............Arlington Hotel.
Stevenson, John W., Kentucky......Riggs House.
Thurman, Allen G., Ohio.................1017 14th street, N. W.
Wadleigh, Bainbridge, New Hamp.-136 Pennsylvania ave., S. E.
Wallace, William A., Pennsylvania-Willard's Hotel.
West, J. R., Louisiana...................815 15th street, N. W.
Whyte, Wm. Pinckney, Maryland--1536 I street, N. W.
Windom, William, Minnesota.........113 Maryland avenue. N. E.
Withers, Robert E., Virginia............Alexandria, Virginia.
Wright, George G., Iowa................326 4½ street, N. W.

ALPHABETICAL LIST OF REPRESENTATIVES WITH THEIR RESIDENCES IN WASHINGTON.

MICHAEL C. KERR, Speaker, Ind.-Willard's Hotel.
Adams, Charles H., New York.........Arlington Hotel.
Ainsworth, Lucien L., Iowa ....509 E street, N. W.
Anderson, William B., Illinois.........476 Pennsylvania avenue.
Ashe, Thomas S., North Carolina ....432 H street, N. W.
Atkins, John D. C., Tennessee ....420 10th street.
Bagby, John C., Illinois ....469 Missouri avenue.
Bagley, George A., New York ....1221 G street, N. W.
Bagley, John H., jr., New York ......Congressional Hotel.
Baker, John H., Indiana................601 E street, N. W.
Baker, William H., New York ....Ebbitt House.
Ballou, Latimer W., Rhode Island...National Hotel.
Banks, Nathaniel P., Massachusetts-814 17th street, N. W.
Banning, Henry B., Ohio...............204 N. J. avenue, S. E.

24

Bass, Lyman K., New York ....1129 14th street, N. W.
Beebe, George M., New York---- ......334 C street, N. W.
Bell, Samuel N., New Hampshire -- National Hotel.
Blackburn, Joseph C. S., Kentucky-Ebbitt House.
Blair, Henry W., New Hampshire--117 Maryland avenue, N. E.
Bland, Richard P., Missouri ....1217 G street, N. W.
Bliss, Archibald M., New York.. --- Arlington Hotel.
Blount, James H., Georgia ....523 13th street, N. W.
Boone, Andrew R., Kentucky ....1309 F street, N. W.
Bradford, Taul, Alabama ....607 13th street, N. W.
Bradley, Nathan B., Michigan ....218 3d street, N. W.
Bright, John M., Tennessee ----- .....411 12th street, N. W.
Brown, John Young, Kentucky ....1013 E street, N. W.
Brown, William R., Kansas ....613 F street, N. W.
Buckner, Aylett H., Missouri ....333 Missouri avenue.
Burchard, Horatio C., Illinois ....Hamilton House.
Burchard, Samuel D., Wisconsin-----211 East Capitol street.
Burleigh, John H., Maine ....Arlington Hotel.
Cabell, George C., Virginia .. .. 1103 G street, N. W.
Caldwell, John H., Alabama ....1202 E street, N. W.
Caldwell, William P., Tennessee......318 Indiana avenue.
Campbell, Alexander, Illinois ....National Hotel.
Candler, Milton A., Georgia ....523 13th street, N. W.
Cannon, Joseph G., Illinois.............National Hotel.
Cason, Thomas J., Indiana ....142 A street, N. E.
Caswell, Lucien B., Wisconsin.........605 13th street, N. W.
Cate, George W., Wisconsin ....220 B street, N. W.
Caulfield, Bernard G., Illinois.........1228 14th street, N. W.
Chapin, Chester W., Massachusetts-Arlington Hotel.
Chittenden, Simeon B., New York---Vt. ave. and H street, N. W.
Clarke, John B., Kentucky.............New York Avenue Hotel.
Clark, John B., jr., Missouri ....426 11th street, N. W.
Clymer, Heister, Pennsylvania.........1536 I street, N. W.
Cochrane, Alex. G., Pennsylvania......717 14th street, N. W.
Collins, Francis D., Pennsylvania---1117 F street, N. W.
Conger, Omar D., Michigan ....National Hotel.
Cook, Philip, Georgia ....511 13th street, N. W.
Cowan, Jacob P., Ohio ....Imperial Hotel.
Cox, Samuel S., New York ....112 East Capitol street.
Crapo, William W., Massachusetts--Wormley's.
Crounse, Lorenzo, Nebraska ....National Hotel.
Culberson, David B., Texas ....226 3d street, N. W.
Cutler, Augustus W., New Jersey ---130 C street, S. E.
Danford, Lorenzo, Ohio ....Willard's Hotel.
Darrall, Chester B., Louisiana.........421 11th street, N. W.
Davis, Joseph J., North Carolina-----1321 14th street, N. W.
Davy, John M., New York.............608 14th street, N. W.
De Bolt, Rezin A., Missouri ....316 C street, N. W.
Denison, Dudley C., Vermont ....130 East Capitol street.
Dibrell, George G., Tennessee.........903 E street, N. W.
Dobbins, Samuel A., New Jersey.....Washington House.

Douglas, Beverly B., Virginia..........515 F street, N. W.
Dunnell, Mark H., Minnesota ....506 E street, N. W.
Durand, George H., Michigan ....National Hotel.
Durham, Milton J., Kentucky..........1331 G street, N. W.
Eames, Benjamin T., Rhode Island..Wormley's.
Eden, John R., Illinois .... Metropolitan Hotel.
Egbert, Albert G., Pennsylvania......Ebbitt House.
Ellis, E. John, Louisiana ....337 C street, N. W.
Ely, Smith, jr., New York ....1310 I street, N. W.
Evans, James L., Indiana ....723 13th street, N. W.
Faulkner, Chas. J., West Virginia...National Hotel.
Felton, William H., Georgia..............National Hotel.
Finley, Jesse J., Florida..................515 12th street, N. W.
Forney, William H., Alabama........ 607 13th street, N. W.
Fort, Greenbury L., Illinois ....511 13th street, N. W.
Foster, Charles, Ohio.. ....1320 F street, N. W.
Franklin, Benjamin J., Missouri.....465 Missouri avenue.
Freeman, Chapman, Pennsylvania..1310 F street, N. W.
Frost, Rufus S., Massachusetts..........Arlington Hotel.
Frye, William P., Maine..................1235 New York avenue.
Fuller, Benoni S., Indiana..............400 3d street, N. W.
Garfield, James A., Ohio................13th and I streets, N. W.
Gause, Lucien C., Arkansas..............National Hotel.
Gibson, Randall L., Louisiana..........1325 K street, N. W.
Glover, John M., Missouri................912 Scott Place.
Goode, John, jr., Virginia ....1103 G street, N. W.
Goodin, John R., Kansas................715 Market Space.
Gunter, Thomas M., Arkansas..........224 3d street, N. W.
Hale, Eugene, Maine ....1408 H street, N. W.
Hamilton, Andrew H., Indiana........Willard's Hotel.
Hamilton, Robert, New Jersey........Willard's Hotel.
Hancock, John, Texas ....National Hotel.
Haralson, Jere, Alabama ....1526 M street, N. W.
Hardenberg, Aug. A., New Jersey..453 C street, N. W.
Harris, Benj. W., Massachusetts......220 A street, S. E.
Harris, Henry R., Georgia..............National Hotel.
Harris, John T., Virginia................Metropolitan Hotel.
Harrison, Carter H., Illinois............935 K street, N. W.
Hartridge, Julian, Georgia............513 13th street, N. W.
Hartzell, William, Illinois..............Metropolitan Hotel.
Hatcher, Robert A., Missouri..........225 3d street, N. W.
Hathorn, Henry H., New York........Arlington Hotel.
Haymond, William S., Indiana........Continental Hotel.
Hays, Charles, Alabama ....732 21st street, N. W.
Hendee, George W., Vermont..........917 G street, N. W.
Henderson, Thomas J., Illinois........419 6th street, N. W.
Henkle, Eli J., Maryland..................Baltimore, Maryland.
Hereford, Frank, West Virginia......1412 I street, N. W.
Hewitt, Abram S., New York............1215 K street, N. W.
Hewitt, Goldsmith W., Alabama......510 13th street, N. W.
Hill, Benjamin H., Georgia ....Congressional Hotel.

Hoar, George F., Massachusetts ......919 I street, N. W.
Hoge, Solomon L., South Carolina...334 C street, N. W.
Holman, William S., Indiana............3d and D streets, N. W.
Hooker, Charles E., Mississippi......511 13th street, N. W.
Hopkins, James H., Pennsylvania......613 13th street, N. W.
Hoskins, George G., New York........Willard's Hotel.
House, John F., Tennessee...............1309 F street, N. W.
Hubbell, Jay A., Michigan ....N. Y. avenue and 13th st.
Hunter, Morton C., Indiana ....Hamilton House.
Hunter, Eppa, Virginia...................1103 G street, N. W.
Hurd, Frank H., Ohio ....Wormley's.
Hurlbut, Stephen A., Illinois............823 Vermont avenue.
Hyman, John A., North Carolina ...1019 4th street, N. W.
Jenks, George A., Pennsylvania......1212 G street, N. W.
Jones, Frank, New Hampshire........Imperial Hotel.
Jones, Thomas L., Kentucky...........121 B street, S. E.
Joyce, Charles H., Vermont ....810 12th street, N. W.
Kasson, John A., Iowa...................1534 I street, N. W.
Kehr, Edward C., Missouri.............1322 G street, N. W.
Kelly, William D., Pennsylvania......715 14th street, N. W.
Ketcham, Winthrop W., Penn..........1342 New York avenue.
Kimball, Alanson M., Wisconsin......Ebbitt House.
King, William S., Minnesota...........1532 I street, N. W.
Knott, J. Proctor, Kentucky...........821 13th street, N. W.
Lamar, Lucius Q. C., Mississippi......520 13th street, N. W.
Landers, George M., Connecticut.....Riggs House.
Landers, Franklin, Indiana ....715 12th street, N. W.
Lane, La Fayette, Oregon ....201 D street, N. W.
Lapham, Elbridge G., New York.....407 East Capitol street.
Lawrence, William, Ohio................Washington House.
Leavenworth, Elias W., New York..Arlington Hotel.
Le Moyne, J. V., Illinois................Ebbitt House.
Levy, William M., Louisiana...........1307 F street, N. W.
Lewis, Burwell B., Alabama...........914 12th street, N. W.
Lord, Scott, New York..................Hamilton House.
Luttrell, John K., California ....516 10th street, N. W.
Lynch, John R. Mississippi ....1419 Pierce Place.
Lynde, William P., Wisconsin.........823 Vermont avenue.
Mackey, E. W. M., South Carolina.1440 M street, N. W.
Mackey, L. A., Pennsylvania..........608 14th street, N. W.
MacDougall, Clinton D., New York.515 12th street, N. W.
Magoon, Henry S., Wisconsin ....233 Pennsylvania avenue.
Maish, Levi, Pennsylvania.............723 14th street, N. W.
McCrary, George W., Iowa............207 D street, N. W.
McDill, James W., Iowa ......412 6th street, N. W.
McFarland, William, Tennessee......511 13th street, N. W.
McMahon, John A., Ohio...............53 D street, S. E.
Meade, Edwin R., New York..........725 15th street, N. W.
Metcalfe, Henry B., New York.......1501 10th street, N. W.
Miller, Samuel F., New York ....Washington House.
Milliken, Charles W., Kentucky......1015 E street, N. W.

Mills, Roger Q., Texas.....................222 3d street, N. W.
Money, Hernando D., Mississippi ...Imperial Hotel.
Monroe, James, Ohio......................810 12th street, N. W.
Morrison, William R., Illinois.........Willard's Hotel.
Morgan, Charles H. Missouri...........506 Maine avenue.
Mutchler, William, Pennsylvania...417 6th street, N. W.
Nash, Charles E., Louisiana...........464 C street, N. W.
Neal, Lawrence T , Ohio.................Ebbitt House.
New, Jeptha D., Indiana.................1224 I street, N. W.
Norton, N. L., New York ....12 Grant Place.
O'Brien, William J., Maryland........Baltimore, Maryland.
Odell, N. Holmes, New York...........725 15th street, N. W.
Oliver, Addison, Iowa ....207 D street, N. W.
O'Neill, Charles, Pennsylvania.......516 13th street, N. W.
Packer, John B., Pennsylvania........Congressional Hotel.
Page, Horace F., California............1325 F street, N. W.
Payne, Henry B., Ohio...................933 New York avenue.
Phelps, James, Connecticut............457 C street, N. W.
Philips, John F., Missouri..............1322 G street, N. W.
Phillips, William A., Kansas.   ...   1008 H street, N. W.
Pierce, Henry L., Massachusetts......Wormley's.
Piper, William A. California ....608 13th street, N. W.
Plaisted, Harris M., Maine ....1106 New York avenue.
Platt, Thomas C., New York...........Arlington Hotel.
Poppleton, Earley F., Ohio............218 A street, S. E.
Potter, Allen, Michigan ....201 East Capitol street.
Powell, Joseph, Pennsylvania .... 1342 New York avenue.
Pratt, Henry O., Iowa ....938 E street, N. W.
Purman, William J., Florida...........144 A street, N. E.
Rainey, Joseph H., South Carolina..1433 L street, N. W.
Randall, Samuel J., Pennsylvania...120 C street, S. E.
Rea, David, Missouri.....................1309 F street N. W.
Reagan, John H., Texas.................226 3d street, N. W.
Reilly, John, Pennsylvania.............215 A street, S. E.
Reilly, James B., Pennsylvania ......205 D street, N. W.
Rice, Americus V., Ohio................Congressional Hotel.
Riddle, Haywood Y., Tennessee......508 13th street, N. W.
Robbins, John, Pennsylvania ....National Hotel.
Robbins, Wm. M., North Carolina..421 11th street, N. W.
Roberts, Charles B., Maryland ....813 Vermont avenue.
Robinson, Milton S., Indiana..........521 13th street, N. W.
Ross, Miles, New Jersey................Ebbitt House.
Ross, Sobieski, Pennsylvania.........1405 F street, N. W.
Rusk, Jeremiah M., Wisconsin........1320 F street, N. W.
Sampson, Ezekiel S., Iowa.............410 6th street, N. W.
Savage, John S., Ohio...................715 14th street, N. W.
Sayler, Milton, Ohio.....................Arlington Hotel.
Scales, Alfred M., North Carolina...1321 New York avenue.
Schleicher, Gustave, Texas............121 B street, S. E.
Schumaker, John G., New York......Arlington Hotel.
Seelye, Julius H., Massachusetts.....1415 G street, N. W.

Sheakley, James, Pennsylvania ......410 6th street, N. W.
Singleton, Otho R., Mississippi.......514 13th street, N. W.
Sinnickson, Clem. H., New Jersey...Hamilton House.
Slemons, William F., Arkansas.......315 New Jersey avenue.
Smalls, Robert, South Carolina......910 14th street, N. W.
Smith, A. Herr, Pennsylvania........Willard's Hotel.
Smith, William E., Georgia............Congressional Hotel.
Southard, Milton I., Ohio.............426 11th street, N. W.
Sparks, William A. J., Illinois.......Metropolitan Hotel.
Spencer, William B., Louisiana......337 C street, N. W.
Springer, William M., Illinois........209 A street, S. E.
Stenger, William S., Pennsylvania..21 Grant Place.
Stevenson, Adlai E., Illinois.........469 Missouri avenue.
Stone, William H., Missouri..........National Hotel.
Stowell, William H. H., Virginia....1212 New York avenue.
Strait, Horace B., Minnesota ....318 C street, N. W.
Swann, Thomas, Maryland ....823 15th street, N. W.
Tarbox, John K., Massachusetts....330 Missouri avenue.
Teese, Frederick H., New Jersey....453 C street, N. W.
Terry, William, Virginia...............206 New Jersey avenue, S. E.
Thomas, Philip F., Maryland.........Gray's, I and 15th streets.
Thompson, Chas. P., Massachusetts..518 13th street, N. W.
Thornburg, Jacob M., Tennessee....226 14th street, S. W.
Throckmorton, James W., Texas....402 6th street, N. W.
Townsend, Martin I., New York .....810 12th street, N. W.
Townsend, Wash., Pennsylvania....621 F street, N. W.
Tucker, J. Randolph, Virginia........1103 G street, N. W.
Tufts, John Q., Iowa...................206 5th street, S. E.
Turney, Jacob, Pennsylvania.........Metropolitan Hotel.
Vance, John L., Ohio...................Metropolitan Hotel.
Vance, Robert B., North Carolina...104 3d street, N. W.
Van Vorhes, Nelson H., Ohio.........19 Grant Place.
Waddell, Alfred M., North Carolina..421 11th street, N. W.
Wait, John T., Connecticut............607 13th street, N. W.
Waldron, Henry, Michigan............National Hotel.
Walker, Charles C. B., New York ...1221 G street, N. W.
Walker, Gilbert C., Virginia...........Willard's Hotel.
Wallace, Alex. S., South Carolina...1921 Pennsylvania avenue.
Wallace, John W., Pennsylvania....324 4½ street, N. W.
Walling, Ansel T., Ohio................723 13th street, N. W.
Walsh, William, Maryland ....1340 I street, N. W.
Ward, Elijah, New York...............1607 H street, N. W.
Warren, Wm. W., Massachusetts....1231 New York avenue.
Wells, Erastus, Missouri..............Willard's Hotel.
Wells, G. Wiley, Mississippi...........1419 G street, N. W.
Wheeler, William A., New York......810 12th street, N. W.
White, John D., Kentucky ....1200 K street, N. W.
Whitehouse, John O., New York.....Willard's Hotel.
Whiting, Richard H., Illinois ....525 13th street, N. W.
Whitthorne, Wash. C., Tennessee ...720 13th street, N. W.
Wigginton, P. D., California...........201 D street, N. W.

Wike, Scott, Illinois...................476 Pennsylvania avenue.
Willard, George, Michigan ....310 Indiana avenue.
Williams, Andrew, New York..........408 6th street, N. W.
Williams, Alpheus S., Michigan......National Hotel.
Williams, Charles G., Wisconsin......18 Grant Place.
Williams, James, Delaware..............510 12th street, N. W.
Williams, James D., Indiana.. ....3d and D streets, N. W.
Williams, Jeremiah N., Alabama ...129 East Capitol street.
Williams, William B., Michigan......218 3d street, N. W.
Willis, Benjamin A., New York......1340 Massachusetts avenue.
Wilshire, William W., Arkansas.....107 Pennsylvania avenue, E.
Wilson, Benjamin, West Virginia...1323 H street, N. W.
Wilson, James, Iowa....................410 6th street, N. W.
Wood, Alan, jr., Pennsylvania..........113 Maryland avenue, N. E.
Wood, Fernando, New York..............825 15th street, N. W.
Woodburn, William, Nevada...........Windsor House.
Woodworth, Laurin D., Ohio...........65 K street, N. E.
Yeates, Jesse J., North Carolina.....409 12th street, N. W.
Young, Casey, Tennessee ....1327 G street, N. W.

TERRITORIAL DELEGATES.

Fenn, S. S., Idaho............................
Cannon, George Q., Utah ....1303 F street, N. W.
Elkins, Stephen B., New Mexico.....1326 Massachusetts avenue.
Jacobs, Orange, Washington..........717 14th street, N. W.
Kidder, Jefferson P. Dakota............National Hotel.
Maginnis, Martin, Montana ....713 14th street, N. W.
Patterson, Thomas M., Colorado......826 12th street, N. W.
Steele, William R., Wyoming ....Ebbitt House.
Stevens, Hiram S., Arizona.............1324 G street, N. W.

CITY DIRECTORY.

EXECUTIVE MANSION,
Pennsylvania avenue, between Fifteenth and Seventeenth streets.

TREASURY DEPARTMENT,
Corner Fifteenth street and Pennsylvania avenue.

DEPARTMENT OF JUSTICE,
Pennsylvania avenue, opposite Treasury Department.

STATE DEPARTMENT,
Corner Seventeenth street and New York avenue.

WAR DEPARTMENT,
Corner Seventeenth street and Pennsylvania avenue.

INTERIOR DEPARTMENT.
F street, between Seventh and Ninth streets.

POST OFFICE DEPARTMENT,
E street, between Seventh and Eighth streets.

DEPARTMENT OF AGRICULTURE,
On the Island, opposite Thirteenth street.

SMITHSONIAN INSTITUTE,
West of the Capitol, opposite Tenth street.

NATIONAL OBSERVATORY,
E street, North, opposite Twenth-third street, West.

ARSENAL,
Foot of Four-and-a half street, southwest of Capitol.

NAVY YARD,
On the Eastern Branch, southeast of Capitol.

CITY HALL,
Four-and-a-half street, Northwest.

WASHINGTON MONUMENT,
One mile directly west of Capitol.

CONGRESSIONAL PRINTING OFFICE,
Corner North Capitol and H streets.

CORCORAN'S ART GALLERY,
Corner Pennsylvania avenue and Seventeenth street.

M. P. RICE,   AMOS I RICE

Photographers,

1217, 1219 Pennsylvania Avenue,

Washington, D. C.

Brady's

National Portrait Gallery,

No. 625 Pennsylvania Avenue,

Between 6th and 7th Sts.

— ◄•► —

Mr. Brady has the pleasure of announcing to his friends and the Public that he has returned to Washington and re-opened his gallery. He will be aided by a corps of the best artists, and will avail himself of all the recent improvements in the photographic art. Mr. Brady will give his personal attention to his patrons daily from 9 a. m. till 5 p. m.

Lafayette House,

EUROPEAN PLAN,

Cor. Second and B Streets, N. W.

Washington, D. C.

— ◆ —

This House is entirely new, is elegantly furnished, and centrally located, being within one block of the Capitol, Botanical Garden, and all the lines of Street Cars.

ROOMS $1.00 TO $1.50 PER DAY.

GEO. DAY, PROPRIETOR.

www.ingramcontent.com/pod-product-compliance
Lightning Source LLC
Chambersburg PA
CBHW021621290326
41931CB00047B/1382